OTHER BOOKS BY SUE MCCOLLUM

Moving On…before and after cancer

Brave and Free

Real Love Stories Have No Endings…

Who Holds the Key?

INTRODUCTION

Sun Valley provides the perfect place to delight in the magic of the Christmas season. Removed from the busyness of our daily lives we can enjoy those simple pleasures of being with our family and friends and enjoying a time of love and fellowship.

This book shares these thoughts with you in poetic rhyme as well as with the delightful artwork of Jane Wooster Scott. Let your heart and mind step back and reflect on the many joys of this season as you as your fingers waltz through the pages of this book.

Sun Valley is a wonderful place to share the joys of Christmas, but wherever you are, may your days be filled with love in your heart, peace in your soul, and joy in your spirit. as you enjoy this magical time of the year

Sue McCollum

TABLE OF CONTENTS

THE MAGIC OF CHRISTMAS

THE HEART OF SUN VALLEY

JOLLY OLD SAINT NICK

THE MANY GIFTS OF CHRISTMAS

THE MAGIC OF CHRISTMAS

DASHING THROUGH THE SNOW...

Sun Valley Inn

Sue McCollum

A Sun Valley Christmas

Christmas in Sun Valley
Is certainly a dream come true.
Fresh snow falling, Christmas lights,
Carolers, and Santa too.

It's like a fairy tale come true
And we are a part of the story
Involved we are for a brief time
In this magical time of glory.

When the cares of the world go away
In our heart is love and joy.
Our minds and spirits are lifted up
A time, in life, to enjoy.

Christmas is a special treat -
To live the Sun Valley dream.
To be in a place of joy and peace
Where beauty and love are seen.

CHRISTMAS PARTIES

The room was full of people
All dressed in their holiday best.
This Sun Valley crowd looked so smart
As if this were a test.

A test to see just how they would do
When no longer on the ski hill were they.
Just how were they going to act tonight?
What would they all have to say?

But Christmas time is special
And our thoughts turn to other things.
Families and friends are now the focus
For that makes our heart sing.

We all came here to downhill ski
But we're connected by so much more.
Our love and concern for each other
And from our hearts this does pour.

I'm thankful for the Christmas parties
Where together we can all be.
To celebrate the Christmas spirit,
A special time for you and me.

MAGIC MOMENTS

Christmas is all about family,
To spend some time together.
In Sun Valley the highlight is skiing
In good or stormy weather.

To ski a few hours is such a treat
To enjoy the great fresh air.
The views, the snow, family, and friends
It's life without a care.

I am so very thankful
I can share this moment in time.
I'll stop my daily routines,
And enjoy this treasure that's mine.

At home, the fireplace is all aglow.
The Christmas tree standing tall.
I'll sit down and chat with the ones I love -
The best Christmas gift of all.

PICTURE PERFECT FAMILY

My Norman Rockwell family
Looks like Andy Warhol to me.
The perfect family I do not have,
For we are all very different I see.

To mix up broken and strong willed people
And expect a 'Rockwell' group to be,
Is an impossible task for us to do
For imperfect humans are we.

But valuable life lessons I can learn
From my family members each day,
If I just sit and listen to them
Hearing what they have to say.

No expectations, no big advice,
But an encouraging and listening ear.
This will help them grow in their life
For, to God and me, they are dear.

So during this holiday season
I'll try to remember to be -
One who accepts each family member
Even if they're not like me.

THE TREE

The tree has been cut and now stands in place
Waiting for the lights to appear.
Challenging it is to string the lights
But we launch ahead without fear.

The box of ornaments we open
With great excitement each year.
For each ornament tells a story
A gift from a loved one that's dear.

The new ornaments certainly sparkle
And give us great delight.
But the old have been there for many years,
And are a beautiful sight.

So our ornaments it seems are just like our friends
They each have a story that's been told.
Some stories are new and fun to hear
But the old stories are just like gold.

OLD ORNAMENTS

"Like friends, the old ornaments mean the most,"
My friend did say to me.
I tumbled this thought around in my brain
And her point, I certainly could see.

The very old ornaments mean the most
For the memories they give to me -
The decorated egg, my son did make,
When he was only three.

The wooden cut ornaments I do treasure
Were made by another son,
These are the ornaments I treasure most
For they were made when he was young.

Other ornaments we have collected
From trips both near and far,
These are the ones that are so precious
For they shine like an evening star.

Those gifts from friends over the years
Are now of great value to me.
For some have gone and all I now have
Is their ornament on my tree.

We have great comfort with our old friends
And with our old Christmas ornaments too.
For they each provide delightful memories
Of the things, in life, we did do.

THE ANNUAL CHRISTMAS PARTY

It's special when old friends gather
To share their lives with each other.
For life is done at such a frantic pace
We rarely have time for our brother.

So to set a time each Christmas season
To stop our busy lives,
To take the time to relax and be
Present with our friends and wives.

To talk about the year gone by
And all that has taken place.
To laugh and cry and hug each other
Away from the frantic pace.

An oasis Sun Valley is for each one
For it provides a moment to just be,
With friends we've known for a long time
To chat, and relax, and – just be.

THE HOLIDAYS

It's all magnified at Christmas time,

The good as well as the bad.

Rejoice we do with our little ones

While others are so very sad.

Heightened emotions we all do have

At this time of the year.

Love and compassion are out there

But also are anger and fear.

Everything is intensified

So perhaps the best thing for me,

Is to not get involved with many new things

But try to relax and just be.

SINGLE AT CHRISTMAS

The singles all meet on Christmas Eve
To keep company with each other.
All have a reason why they're not with
A husband, wife, or their mother.

Perhaps it's a blessing in disguise
For with friends they don't need to hear
The same old stories again and again
Told year after year after year.

No ribbing do they have to take
From that family member again -
That reddens their face and causes them
Embarrassment and chagrin.

Away from the family tension
Of getting Christmas presents – just right.
The little quarrels that go on and on
Often far into the night.

So singles, when you gather,
Click your glasses with good cheer.
For you're with your chosen group of friends
Those who to you are dear.

HOLIDAY STRESS

The holidays seem to magnify
Just where we are in life.
Are we at peace within our heart
Or are we filled with anger and strife?

Families do gather, gifts we all buy,
There is so much we have to do.
Then stress and anxiety do enter in
And that affects both me and you.

The holiday season should be filled with joy
But so much pressure it seems to bring,
Do I need to buy that one more gift?
Do they need another thing?

Perhaps I need to step back
And not be upset and shout,
For love, joy and peace within our heart
Is what Christmas is all about.

THE HEART OF SUN VALLEY

SUE McCOLLUM

SKIING BALDY MOUNTAIN

When the chair lift opens we are there
And up Baldy Mountain we go -
Hats, goggles, and scarves cover us up
So who sits beside us - we don't know.

But to be the first one down the mountain
Is certainly a dream come true,
The runs are groomed to perfection
And we have fresh snow to ski through.

There are many runs to choose from
And each one is so unique
Depending on our mood for the day
And how much challenge we seek.

We meet at Seattle Ridge for lunch
And we all have so much to say -
Christmas Ridge was great, Mayday Bowl divine
And we felt the Limelight burn today.

Tired we all are for we never stop
But a few more runs we do make.
A glorious day we all have had
And great memories home - we now take.

THE OPENING

She was all a glow when I saw her
For her dream had, at last, come true.
The new Lodge at Dollar Mountain
Had been named for her too.

Years it was in the planning,
Not a detail was past by.
Bold and beautiful, in every way
It made all visitors sigh.

The opening was magnificent -
Ice sculptures, and Santa too.
The wide-eyed children watching the Carolers
Singing Christmas carols as they do.

Feeding the entire Valley
Was indeed a generous thing,
But the highlight of the evening was
When Carol made the bell to ring.

The torch light parade down the mountain
Was a treat for one and all.
How do they ski with a torch in both hands
And never have a fall?

Yes, the opening of Carol's Dollar Lodge
Was perfect in every way.
We'll all have delicious memories to savor
At the end of this perfect day.

Carol Holding opening Carol's Dollar Lodge
12.20.05

TORCHLIGHT PARADE

Christmas eve at the Sun Valley Lodge
There are cookies and hot chocolate for all.
It is indeed a festive event
Where everyone has a ball.

First there is the ice show,
A beautiful treat for the eye.
Children and professionals all skate
Such talent does make you sigh.

The Carolers sing and Santa does come.
The children are thrilled as are we.
To see Santa come in a sleigh
And also skate beautifully.

The torchlight parade down Baldy Mountain
Is truly a spectacular sight.
Then fireworks illuminate the dark black sky
Which concludes this wonderful night.

THE SUN VALLEY LODGE

Dinner at the Lodge was perfect.
The dining room beautiful to the eye.
The hustle and bustle of all the help -
Festive dress that makes one sigh.

The carolers sang their Christmas carols,
Then Santa came to call.
Adults and children all around
Everyone had a ball.

A trio played music for dancing.
The dance floor was full indeed.
Couples and children all did dance
Taking turns as to who would lead.

The food was delicious, the service fine,
An evening to savor forever.
Christmas Eve at the Sun Valley Lodge
Is a time we all will treasure.

ONE OF THE BOYS

"I'm just one of the boys,"

he did say

As I spoke to him

The other day.

"It's my staff

I give the credit to,

For they all excel

In what they do."

But he makes sure their job gets done

With his training and planning each day.

Pleasing the people, who come to dine,

In his very own special way.

A loyal employee for many years,

Just one of the boys is he.

If the whole world could only be one of the boys,

What a better world it would be.

Thanks Claude

Carol's Dollar Lodge

It is perfect in all aspects.
Not a detail was over looked.
Carol's Dollar Lodge, in Sun Valley,
Will certainly be permanently booked.

It's built for teaching young children
Just how to ski today -
A magic carpet to take them up
So skiing down can be like play.

The instructors all are very kind.
They are patient and helpful too.
Inspiring confidence, in the children,
In all they say and do.

Everything is built, child size -
The tables, wash sinks, and chairs.
It's a fairyland for children;
…It's life without a care.

The parents are very thrilled for
The children are having fun.
A delicious way to spend your vacation
Under the Sun Valley sun.

THE HEART OF SUN VALLEY

How do we thank the Holding's
For all that they have done?
For they've created this magical place
Under the Sun Valley sun.

Each thing that they have done
Has been done with thought and style,
Bike paths, hiking, physical things,
Or a bench to rest awhile.

The ski lodges on the mountain,
Are beautiful to behold.
We're grateful you do own them
And that they will never be sold.

Privileged we are to have you.
You have done all things, just right.
The Sun Valley Lodge, now beautiful,
All seasons a delightful sight.

Little by little we've seen your mark,
Improving things as you go.
You're making Sun Valley a family place,
Safe for our children to grow.

You've both left your stamp on this place,
For many years to come.
Thank you for making Sun Valley the place
Where we can relax and have fun.

Thank you, Carol and Earl Holding

JOLLY OLD SAINT NICK

Wilber Is Impersonating Santa Again!
© Wooster Scott

SANTA CLAUS

- They err who think Santa Claus comes down the chimney,
he really enters through the heart!

Yes there is a Santa Clause
Who is with us every day.
He lives deep down within our heart
And guides us along our way.

He doesn't come just once a year,
But he is always there,
To lead, to guide, to bring us joy
Because for us he does care.

It's that happy, healthy spirit
He brings at Christmas time,
The love and joy and giving to us
That makes our heart and soul shine.

Yes, Santa is here all year long
For he lives within our heart.
To love us as well as to love others
So from Santa we'll never part.

CHRISTMAS FANTASY

Christmas is a time to dream
For folks both old and young
To leave behind our daily routine
To laugh and to have fun.

To pretend there is a Santa Clause
Who will make this world just right -
He'll fill the world with love and peace
And also with joy and delight.

For just a season every year
We move to this fantasyland,
To all be children, once again,
And life is oh, so grand.

So Santa is just the symbol
Of a world where we want to live,
A world with dreams of goodness and love
And from our hearts we can give.

Santa's Here

We all gather at the back of the Lodge
For Santa will be here soon.
Mulled cider, cookies, and hot cocoa are there
And often a full moon too.

It's a party given by the Sun Valley Company.
There are treats and entertainment for all.
An ice show and the torchlight parade -
The children, young and old, have a ball.

Then pulled by many elves on skates,
Santa, in the red suit, appears.
Around the rink he does go,
As the audience waves and cheers.

He stops to sit upon his throne
To hear from all who are there.
He listens intently to each little child
Because Santa for each one does care.

This is a great Sun Valley tradition -
This magical Christmas Eve night.
A mixer for the entire community
That fills us all with delight.

Thanks, Sun Valley Company

Jolly Old Saint Nick

No one ever told Santa
That his red suit is out of date.
That he must work, by the clock,
And never show up late.

Perhaps he should contact Weight Watchers
And work on that tummy of his;
No one today has a tummy that size
Unless he's in show biz.

And who does travel by reindeer today
In an open bright red sled -
Flying through the sky, late at night,
While the world is all in bed?

But would Christmas be the same
If the jolly old man was slim -
Driving a brand new four wheel drive
And his helpers were all grown men?

No, I think the wonder of Santa
To those both young and old,
Is to believe in the magic he does give
As for years it has been told.

What's Important at Christmas?

Christmas is a time

To stop, reflect, and see,

Where I've been, where I'm going,

And what's important to me.

Family and friends are important indeed

During this holiday season.

They are the ones that give to me

Love, joy, and a reason…

To move forward each and every day

Being the best that I can be,

For it's my family I learn lessons from

And they learn, as well, from me.

So as we gather this Christmas,

I'll be very aware each day,

To love, encourage, and listen to them

And what they have to say.

CHRISTMAS DAY

Christmas day we all went skiing
And surprised we were to see,
The man who on Christmas Eve
Was climbing down chimneys.

He was smiling and carving some very quick turns
As down the mountain he did go.
People all stopped to look at him
For he was putting on quite a show.

How can he work all night,
And ski all day as well
Handing out candy canes to the children
As they listen to the stories he would tell?

Behind that tummy, the red suit, and beard,
Just who is this man we see?
He brings great joy to all he knows
And is as jolly as he could be.

THE MANY GIFTS OF CHRISTMAS

One Gift

If I had just one gift to give
What would that gift be?
Would it be things of this old world
Or intangible things you can't see?

The greatest and the very best gift
That I could give to you
Would be a faith in the Living God
Who would always be with you.

For things of this world will all disappear.
They wear out, rust out, and get old.
But things of Spirit grow richer each day -
Precious things that can never be sold.

Love, joy, and peace - hope for each day -
This is what God does see.
A faith in Him will never wear out
But will last for eternity.

It's Christmas Magic

At Christmas time we can all be children
Filled with the joy of life.
Love and goodness are all around
And we live in peace – not strife.

Concerned for others we all are.
What can I give them this year?
What will say I love you,
And to me you are so dear.

Decorating the perfect Christmas tree
Is always great fun to do.
For each ornament has a story to tell,
Be they very old or brand new.

Hot cider, cookies, and gingerbread houses
Are all a part of the day.
Carolers singing and children bringing
Their gifts in their own way.

It's a magical, mystical time each year
Where troubles are put at bay.
To spend time with our family and loved ones
And hear what they have to say.

b.b.

Two great loves he does have,
And he excels at both of them.
Skiing and designing beautiful clothes
And both, for him, are a win.

The best mogul skier that ever was –
His arms would fly high above his head,
Crashing down the steepest mountains,
"He's the greatest," everyone has said.

He designed THE SKI, which was innovative and new,
And skiing became easier for all.
But he is also known for his beautiful clothing,
Special pieces – not sold in a mall.

THE SKI and his clothes do last forever
For they are made with precision and care.
The men love his ski's, the women his clothes,
For they have style, function, and flair.

Great ski's – great clothes.
bobbie burns • 271 E. Sun Valley Rd. • Ketchum

MY FIRST CHRISTMAS

(As told to my Grandma)

I know Christmas is more than red hats

And trains under the Christmas tree.

Christmas celebrates the birth of Jesus;

That's what Mom has whispered to me.

As time goes by I'll understand that

But this first Christmas there is much to see.

Lights, ornaments, packages, and ribbons -

It's almost too much for me.

But my favorite thing about Christmas

Is to be with my family

My Grandparents, Cousins, Aunts, and Uncles

And of course that includes me.

It's a festive time of the year

And there are so many things to be done.

But the real reason we celebrate, my Mom has said,

Is the birth of Jesus, God's son.

CHRISTMAS SHOPPING

I saw her Christmas shopping
Just the other day.
What a beautiful woman,
In my mind, I did say.

Blond hair and a flashing smile,
Cheerful and charming was she.
Returning a gift for her child,
She struck up a conversation with me.

We talked about children,
And the challenges they do face.
"My child is in family therapy,
Because of my divorce case."

"She thinks this way and I think that,
So counseling is what we do.
My little girl is so confused
If I were her - I'd be too."

Once again it confirms to me
That behind each smiling face,
Is a story perhaps of anguish and tears
But hidden in the Christmas race.

A hug is what I gave her
As we did part that day.
My heart could feel all her pain
As we left and went our way.

GIFT BOOKS

It's been a classic store in Ketchum
For oh, so many years.
Chock full of all the latest books
That brings joy as well as tears.

The owner is also a classic
With her soft blond hair and smile.
It's a cozy little bookstore
Where you want to stay awhile.

Local authors and big names too
She squeezes into her store.
It's fun to go to a book signing here
And meet the author at the door.

It's now a landmark in Ketchum,
In fact it is renown,
So be sure to go there when Christmas shopping
For it's a favorite place in town.

Chapter One • Main Street • Ketchum

CHRISTMAS TIME

Expectations are running high;

Emotions are at their peak.

Stressed we are, by doing too much,

Just what are we trying to seek?

To be loved unconditionally is what we want,

To be accepted and acknowledged by all.

But human we are and faults we all have,

So often we stumble and fall.

Fall back into old habits,

Not being all we were met to be -

Our human nature pulls us down

And that is a shame to see.

So, back we go to start again,

Keeping our eyes on what's true.

Love, joy, and peace within my heart,

I want that for me - and you.

THAT SPECIAL GIFT

It's a visual treat for the eye,

And it ignites your heart and soul too.

Packed full of unique and special things

This store is a delight to walk through.

Gifts and furnishings from all over the world,

This owner has a great eye.

The manner in which she sets up her store

Makes all who enter sigh.

It's not a quick stop when you go there

To select that special gift,

For there are so may items to choose from

And each one, to your eye, you must lift.

This store, like it's owner, is very distinctive,

An encounter you don't want to miss.

You'll find that unique present you're looking for

Then can cross that off your list.

Bellissimo • The Galleria • Ketchum

My Perfect Christmas

I do love Christmas because
It's so imperfect, you see.
All the plans and thoughts I've had
Get jumbled up as they can be.

At my 'perfect' Christmas dinner party
Aunt Tillie tipped over her wine.
I burned the roast, the potatoes were cold
But the guest thought – all was fine.

The 'perfect' sweaters I did buy
Did not fit – no not one.
The toys I got for the kids
They did not think they were fun.

But each New Year I start once again
Planning that 'perfect' holiday.
But I think that will never ever happen
So I'll just enjoy Christmas day.

Acknowledgments

Thank you, Jane Wooster Scott, for sharing your delightful art work illustrating the magic of the Christmas season in Sun Valley. Your work has long been a part of the fabric that weaves Sun Valley together in a fresh and delightful way. Your ability to depict the joys of life in Sun Valley does enhance the poetic thoughts in this book and I do thank you.

The proceeds from the sale of this book with be given to:

My Blue Dots
www.mybluedots.org
My Blue Dots supports cancer programs
as well as cancer research.